THE HACKY SACK BOOK

IN THEIR CONTINUING STRUGGLE WITH THE forces of gravity, John Cassidy and Diane Waller (author & illustrator of the best-selling *Juggling for the Complete Klutz*) have taken the battle down to their feet. ("For us, footbag games were the next logical step").

Having taught the fine art of juggling to hundreds of thousands of American klutzes ("Many of them practically hopeless"), Cassidy and Waller set forth in *The Hacky Sack Book* to instruct in the New American Footbag Games, the primary object of which is to keep the Hacky Sack footbag up off the ground — using only your feet.

The Hacky Sack Book by Cassidy and Waller is carried out with their characteristic disregard for normal standards of English usage and instruction. As one enthused reader has put it: "Finally, a book written at my speed — reverse."

Acknowledgement

Grateful acknowledgement is hereby registered with those who keep track of kind deeds for the coaching, inspiration, example, and consolation provided by John Stalberger, Iggy & Cruze, Mag Hughes, Billy Haynes, Greg Cortopassi, Bruce Guettich, and the rest of the Kenncorp people.

And to John Snow who took me off the streets.

THE HACKY-SACK BOOK

An illustrated

guide to the

New American

Footbag Games

By John Cassidy

Illustrated by Diane Waller

Klutz Press ● Palo Alto, California

Hacky Sack® is a registered trademark of Kenncorp Sports Incorporated, Vancouver, Washington, and is meant to refer to their Hacky Sack® brand footbag. Use of the trademark Hacky Sack® in this publication is under an arrangement with Kenncorp Sports Inc. Activities described in the following text are meant to be performed with the Hacky Sack® brand footbag. These activities, properly described as the New American Hacky Sack® Footbag Games are occasionally referred to by the trademark Hacky Sack® in the interests of readability. And for the same purposes, the trademark Hacky Sack® is occasionally used in reference to the Hacky Sack® brand footbag.

ISBN 0-932592-05-8

Published by

KLUTZ PRESS
2170 Staunton Court
Palo Alto, CA 94306

Individual copies of this book as well as assorted flying apparatus may be ordered directly from the publisher. See back pages for details.

"Feets don't fail me now."
— *Steppen Fetchit*

" **H**ACKY-SACK" IS A FOOTSPORT; THAT IS, you're going to need feet to play it. The object is to keep the Hacky Sack footbag off the ground using only your lower body. Once the five basic kicks are learned, a whole series of games become possible. Some of them are competitive, like "net-sack", a footbag version of volleyball. Others are cooperative, like "Hacky-circles", in which a group passes the Hacky Sack footbag around by footpower alone.

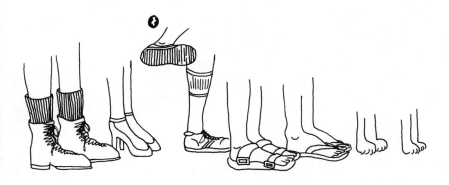

The game has distant relatives in a number of Asian countries, most notably Malaysia, Singapore and the Phillippines, but the American footbag games were developed in Oregon nearly ten years ago by John Stalberger, an athlete/physical therapist looking for a game that would help strengthen a damaged knee. Over the course of several years, Stalberger designed the Hacky Sack footbag and began exploring the limits of his exercise turned game.

Nowadays, hundreds of thousands of Hacky Sack footbag players have demonstrated the phenomenal potential the sport possesses. Andy Linder, for example, from Geneva, Illinois, has executed some 28,234 consecutive kicks. For almost five hours he never allowed the footbag to touch the ground.

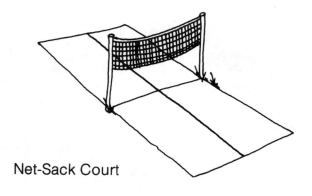

Net-Sack Court

Net-sack, a footbag variation of volleyball played on a court with a five foot net, has evolved into a whiplash-quick game with marathon rallies and a wicked repertoire of sets and spikes.

Meanwhile, in a more cooperative spirit, "Hacky-circles" sized two to twenty-five have become commonplace on schoolyards, campuses and sidewalks everywhere; all part of a National Flying Footbag Syndrome.

Only a few ounces in weight, Hacky Sack footbags must be the world record holder in the fun per cubic centimeter category. They can be taken anywhere and have become especially popular with backpackers, climbers, kayakers and the like — active people frequently outdoors and necessarily light travelers.

At least some of the attraction that the sport holds for its enthusiasts is in its novel emphasis on footskills. In the United States we're not used to thinking of our feet as being particularly skilled in anything, except perhaps getting us down the field, court, or road. In American sports, feet are the hard-working blue-collar types, just doing their job while the hands get all the credit.

With the growing popularity of soccer, a lot of that is changing, but Hacky Sack footbag games are the first to really focus on controlled foot movements. And the potential turns out to be amazing. Feet are not the clod-hoppers we've been led to believe. Their sports stardom has been stifled by the powerful hand, finger and arm lobby.

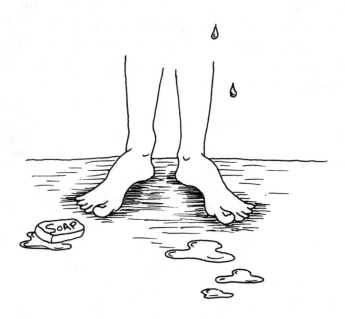

The American Sportsfeet

Rarely understood, frequently undervalued,
but always under you.

From a beginner's point of view, it's this discovery that provides the most excitement. It seems hopeless, trying to get your feet to execute controlled motions, like trying to teach your dog to answer the phone. But then, incredibly, a few kicks start to click and suddenly you're the marvel of the neighborhood.

And after the initial breakthrough, the excitement of being on the best side of a fun learning curve begins. What was impossible yesterday becomes almost routine today.

Probably the most encouraging sign comes just a few days after starting out, after many tears and scenes of bleak frustration. Without really changing your kicks in any way, you'll suddenly start to find the footbag popping up more regularly. It soon reaches the point where you may hesitate to call it skill, but it can't be luck either, it's happening too often.

It's called finding out where your feet are.

Everybody knows where to find their hands. You can catch a ball without looking, you're able to reach for things in the dark. You *know* the length of your arm. We're all unconsciously trained that way.

But feet we're not so sure of. We know they're down there somewhere, at the ends of our legs, but more precisely than that...it's hard to say.

When you start out in footbag games you're going to notice this lack instantly, and for a while it'll be a major source of aggravation. But eventually the foot-to-brain channel will clear up and you'll get a general fix on the podiatric locale situation.

"Hacky-Sack" is a full-on sport, demanding the same kind of discipline and practice one would normally associate with any ball or racket game. There are no mirrors or hidden wires, nor are there any trade secrets I can reveal to make you an instant expert.

But while this fact may be frustrating in the early stages, it also provides the source of the game's long-term attraction, because the full mastery of its skills is an endless challenge. The jump from beginner to cosmic master is no single bound, but an endless set of steps, each one a little achievement of its own, a resting place to enjoy the game from, and a vantage point with a tantalizing view of the next move.

EQUIPMENT

(1) *Feet.* Most any size will do. Two seems to be the best number.

(2) *Shoes.* Leather court shoes are definitely the most popular. Running shoes and canvas tennis shoes can be used, but they're a bit harder to work with — less flat surface area. Sandals and bare feet are next to impossible.

(3) *Hacky Sack footbag.* The material of your footbag is entirely split-grain cowhide and is designed to last a lifetime of hard knocks. Like any leather good, your Hacky Sack footbag will go through a breaking-in period while the material loses its stiffness. You can hasten this somewhat by soaking it for a few seconds in warm water and then working in a few drops of leather dressing, neat's foot oil or the like.

Once your footbag has taken its share of kicks, and has gotten that "properly aged" feel, you can help preserve it by repeating the dressing application from time to time.

EMOTIONAL PREPARATION

Going back for a moment you'll remember that the basic object of this sport is to keep the footbag up off the ground, using only your lower body.

Yes.

Well, ironically enough, that is precisely what is *not* going to happen, certainly not in the early stages. Your footbag may spend brief periods of time soaring through the air, but almost always at great speeds and rarely under any semblance of control. Afterwards the ground is where you will most frequently be able to locate your "Hacky Sack."

At this point there may possibly be a few readers who naively expect that they will somehow be held exempt from this law of universal klutzhood. Not for them the indignities of life as a bungling beginner.

They are, unfortunately, dreaming. *Nobody* picks up footbag games immediately. (For those of you who have ever pondered the essential nature of truth, you need look no further than that last line.)

●

Given the fact that your first few sessions with the footbag are going to be something less than 100% successful, how you prepare yourself for the inevitable ego-battering becomes critical.

Following are a few pointers to help you:

(1) Recognize that the bottom of any learning curve is one of life's least dignified stations. There is little room for pride. None, in fact.

(2) Also recognize that things do not appear difficult from the bottom of this process, they appear utterly impossible. Ignore this perception.

(3) Finally, remember that although you may be bad now, you will never be any worse. (I'm not sure this is any consolation, but I'll pass it on anyway.)

(4) A corollary of the above. Despite all the evidence of your senses, you *will* get better. Trust me. After a couple of little breakthroughs, the first pair of consecutive kicks or the first incredible save,

you'll barely remember those first few faltering steps, beginning with...

THE KICKS

STEP ZERO: The Freestyle Pick-up

Starting out in the footbag games you'll soon be discovering a rich and varied number of ways to make mistakes: over-reaching, under-reaching, shanks, pulls, slices, and, of course, flat-out misses. After each you'll have the opportunity to stoop over, retrieve the footbag and start all over. This can be a humiliating chore, or you can take a more positive attitude and develop a new little art form, THE FREESTYLE PICK-UP.

First and most obvious, of course, is *The Basic*, that is, leaning over from the waist and actually grasping

the footbag with your hand, followed by a straightening up motion. Go ahead and perfect this, but don't be afraid to experiment; use your knees, elbows, teeth...and your imagination.

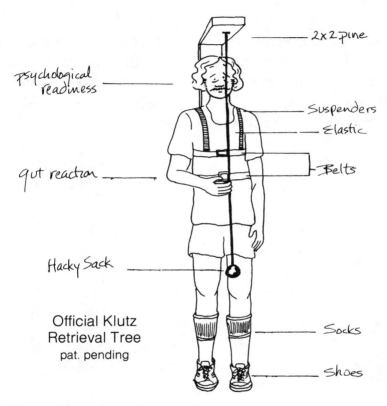

STEP ONE: Stretching

Footbag games involve a number of moves and postures that are going to be completely new, both to you and your legs, and it makes sense to spend a moment stretching before you get started.

Cross your legs and slowly lean over to where you can touch your toes or to where you start to hurt — whichever comes first. Hold there for a five count. Repeat a few times, alternating between right leg crossed over left and vice versa.

Next balance yourself on one foot while holding the other. Flamingoes do this, sort of. Pull your foot slowly up — to your waist if you're the flexible type, somewhere short of that if you're not. Again, hold for a five count and repeat, alternating feet.

STEP TWO: The Inside Kick

The Inside Kick is probably the most basic of the five kicks that you'll be learning. You'll have to get it down to just about 100% reliable before you can really expect to start keeping the footbag in the air very long.

Just for the record, the Inside Kick is meant to be taken whenever the footbag is dropping in front of you and between your shoulders.

You should start by just standing there, relaxed, preferably out of view of any younger brothers or sisters or anyone else liable to get a chuckle out of this, and slowly bring your foot up to about knee high or a little better. Look at the illustration for what I mean. This is a *vertical* lifting motion, your foot comes straight off the ground. Turn your ankle in so that the inside of your foot becomes flatter. It might help to scrunch up your toes. Your support leg has got to be flexed and your weight shifted onto the ball of your foot. Lean over from the waist just a bit for balance.

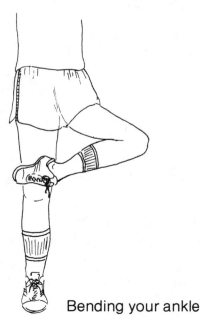

Bending your ankle

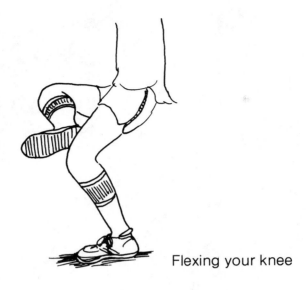

Flexing your knee

Do this motion a couple of times (don't bother with the footbag just yet). Be sure to alternate feet. Think about two things:

(1) Flex your support leg, and

(2) Turn your ankle in to get that flat surface

Obviously you can't go on very long like this but give it a couple of tries, going back and forth between feet. Once you involve the footbag you'll have a tendency to forget all the pointers in your frenzy to just get a foot on the thing — and this can have long-term bad effects. So try to build the good habits in now, while you're still young and impressionable.

All right, you've done the stretching and gone through the motions a couple of times. You're looking good without the footbag. You're ready.

Take the Hacky Sack footbag in your hand and get into the relaxed mode, knees loose. Take a moment to reflect on the fact that the footbag is up off the ground at this particular moment. It may not seem like much now, but you'll soon grow to appreciate this little fact. Toss the thing about as high as your head and about one stride directly in front of you, so that you'll take a small step with your support leg and then bring the kicking foot up underneath the footbag in the same way we've been practicing. Your intention should not be to shoot the footbag off in some outward bound direction, but to just block or bump it back up to yourself. The work "kick" in fact is a little misleading, particularly when we normally associate it with 65 yard punts. What you're actually practicing here is the inside block/bump, or bump/block, or maybe just BLUMP. Anyway, you get the idea.

With your first couple of tries chances are you'll miss the thing entirely, or, failing that, slice it off at some radical angle.

It's guaranteed.

Just relax though. Practice a free-style pick-up and try again. You're doing something your foot and leg have probably never even dreamed of before, so give them a chance.

There is one pointer here that is absolutely critical, and it is the one most easily forgotten, so I'm going to underline it. <u>You've got to concentrate every ounce of visual energy you have on the footbag.</u> From the moment it leaves your hand to the moment it rolls under the couch. Every inch of the way. When it hits your shoe (on the happy chance it does) you've got to know exactly where — what precise little smudge spot. Ask yourself, after every try, "Where did it hit my shoe?"

This is such an important point that I've created a little poem to help you remember. It goes:

"Roses are red,
Violets are blue,
I wonder where the Hacky Sack
Hit my foot."

I hope it helps.

In any event, practice for a few minutes, going back and forth between feet, flexing your support knee, watching the footbag like a hawk, reciting my poem, and working on those freestyles. If everything goes perfectly, the footbag will pop up directly off the inside of your foot — you'll catch it and marvel at your incredible foot-eye coordination.

If everything goes about normally, you'll be all over

the room, digging the footbag out of flowerpots and dog dishes.

Don't despair. Give it ten minutes or so and come back. I think I can probably tell you what you're doing wrong.

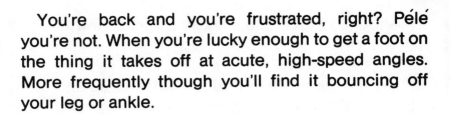

You're back and you're frustrated, right? Pélé you're not. When you're lucky enough to get a foot on the thing it takes off at acute, high-speed angles. More frequently though you'll find it bouncing off your leg or ankle.

My advice is this: Slow down. You're coming up underneath it too soon. Everybody does it. In America, when we kick something, we like to whale on it. You can't do that in Hacky Sack. It may be a footsport, but it's a delicate footsport. Bring your foot up and just bump it. And take a careful look at your tosses. It's hard enough without having to make adjustments for strange throws. (Imagine a peach basket, on the ground, directly in front of the middle of your body about one medium stride; every throw ought to be a dead-on ringer.)

If you started making regular contact and found the footbag generally taking off to the outside of your body, chances are excellent you're (a) contacting too soon and/or (b) not turning up your ankle.

Take it slow. Scrunch up your toes to help with the ankle bend. Take the little step forward and flex your support knee. The whole thing looks a bit like the first half of a curtsy.

Try it for a little longer and then take a break. Stick your Hacky Sack footbag in your pocket and pull it out from time to time during the day, even if only for a couple of kicks. If you take your practice in short-term sprints rather than marathons, you'll learn just as quickly and at the same time keep the frustration level down to something manageable.

After having tried your Inside Kicks for a few minutes you will be irrevocably certain of two things:

(1) Your feet and eyes do not communicate, they live in totally different parts of your body; they have never met.

(2) A normal person would find nothing particularly difficult about footbag games. Over the course of a few minutes he'd progress easily, in a series of smooth, error-free steps, from beginner to expert.

Naturally you're concerned and upset by these two facts. You try a couple more kicks. No improvement.

It's time to get serious.

You throw off extra clothing, grit your teeth, strain every muscle and take a mighty swing at it.

Whiff.

You're beaten. You're red-faced, tear-stained, fist-pounding frustrated.

It's time for some reinforcements.

THE PARTNER SYSTEM

Go find a friend. A fellow Hacky Sack'er with vast amounts of patience, tact and humor would be ideal, but take what you can get. This is what you're going to do.

Your friend is going to stand there a few yards away from you and toss the footbag in gentle, easy arcs that would hit the ground about one step in front of you — except for the fact that you're going to be stepping forward with your support foot and bumping the footbag back with an Inside Kick. (Note: Don't let him throw directly *at* your feet, you want the throws to lead you by a step.)

Emphasize to your friend that this is just batting practice. You want soft, perfectly placed lobs. You will probably discover that bumping the footbag back to your friend is quite a bit easier than popping it straight back to yourself. You might even begin to feel the first faint flush of false confidence.

Switch back and forth between feet; this is a two foot sport. Concentrate on your weaker foot now before you build a bad one-side-only habit.

Despite the fact that this pitch-and-bump-back exercise is a good one for building up some confidence and foot coordination, it has a serious drawback; it's boring, particularly for the guy doing the pitching.

There exists, however, a clever way to get around this problem, and at the same time, get yourself a partner.

Just about the time your friend looks to be fading, suggest that the two of you try passing it back and forth, foot-to-foot. Suggest further that whoever picks up a grounded footbag has to pitch it back to his partner's inside kick, rather than try to kick it back himself.

The effect of this little ploy will soon be obvious; it's actually nothing more than the old pitch-and-bump-back drill, each of you taking turns pitching and kicking. The likelihood of your actually being *able* to pass it back and forth at this early stage is slim, but that shouldn't really matter. You're both getting the practice you need, your partner's been deluded into thinking this is no longer a drill, and who knows, you might even complete a pass or two.

★ HELP WANTED ★

Friendly, tolerant, very patient person (m) or (f) wanted. Some experience in tossing small objects preferred. Flexible hours.

Send resumé and shoe size to: Box 2297 Hackensack N.J.

STEP-TWO-AND-A-HALF: The Minor Kicks, Knee & Toe

The most important thing to know about using these two kicks is not to — unless you really have no choice. Both of them are insidiously tempting, their motions are familiar and natural, but neither has a very big role to play in the footgames.

The Knee Kick

Look at the illustrations for an idea of what I'm talking about. The knee kick is meant to be used only to deflect upwards a low angle pass to your mid-body (in solo consecutives you'll rarely need it). You have to bring your leg up with enough force to set up an Inside or Outside Kick. The temptation is to just bump the footbag down and in front of you, setting up a toe kick, but this tactic is doomed, I can vouch from experience. Your only hope is to use some lift and

The Toe Kick

follow with a controlled kick, either Inside or Outside.

The toe kick is the wild card in footbag games, very tempting to try but no telling where it'll end up. When you're beginning to try consecutives and your Inside and Outside Kicks are spraying all over the place, you'll find yourself lunging all the time for desperate toe kicks. Everybody does it but nobody gets very satisfactory results. My own favorite used to be the fly-back-and-bonk-nose syndrome.

Recognize that toe kicks are last resort measures. If you can step forward and quickly take an Inside, or turn and reach for an Outside, you'll have much better results.

STEP THREE: The Outside Kick

Perfecting the Inside Kick to the point where it always pops vertically back off your foot takes some time. If you keep the various pointers I mentioned in mind and concentrate, you'll get it eventually, despite all the evidence to the contrary.

But even before you get to that stage, you can start working on the next step, your Outside Kick. It'll add variety to your practice sessions, start to make possible some effort at consecutive kicks, and you'll discover a whole new set of mistakes you never even dreamed of before.

The Outside Kick is taken when the Hacky Sack footbag passes to the outside of your shoulders in an arc that hits the ground at a point beside you or just behind you.

I've already nagged you about the most important point in footbag games, watching the Hacky Sack right down to your foot, so I'll pass on that and get into the motion.

Try this a few times without the footbag. Shift your weight onto the ball of one foot entirely, put an arm out to steady yourself, and bring your other foot slowly up, as in the illustration. Your support leg has got to be flexed.

The first thing you will probably notice is that you've never done anything like this before in your life. It doesn't even seem like a kick. It's more a lifting action, reminiscent of the canine-meets-fire-hydrant reflex.

One of the trickiest parts about this move is keeping your kicking foot flat, since there's a real tendency to point the toes down. To counteract that, make the move as slow and deliberate as you can, concentrating on the angle of your foot. It might help to stretch your toes out, the opposite of what you've been doing on your Inside Kicks.

Go through the motion a few times, alternating feet as always. Lean away from the kick, bending your support leg, lifting up a *flat* kicking foot and putting out a balance arm (à la John Travolta).

When you think you've got a rough idea of the kick, go ahead and try it with the footbag. Make nice easy arc tosses with your opposite hand (as in right kicking foot, left tossing hand). They should be aimed at an imaginary peach basket directly off to your side approximately one step. Less than that will cramp the kick and make it even more difficult to keep your foot flat.

You'll soon be re-experiencing the unguided flying footbag syndrome. Relax.

Slow down between tosses, and slow down your kicks. There's an almost irresistible urge to chop at the footbag or take a footswipe at it. You can tell when this is your problem because (a) the footbag will rocket off at flat angles and (b) your balance will be thrown off. You ought to be able to lift your foot up and then put it slowly back down, right where it came from, staying balanced all the while. (Read that last line again, it's the key one.)

The Most Common
Outside Kick Mistakes

The Wind-Up and Swing

This is a batting motion. You lift your foot up and swing it with an upper body twist. Bad idea.

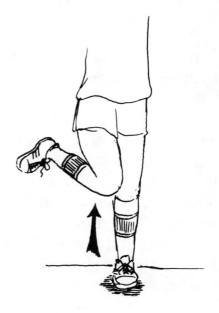

The Jam-Up

The lazy man's outside kick. It happens when you don't step away from the footbag. Makes your foot practically impossible to flatten out. Very awkward.

Since some of your throws will undoubtedly be off the mark, you might as well make the best of that by learning how to make adjustments. Playing in a circle or over a net, you won't see a whole lot of soft, perfectly placed lobs; you'll be moving all the time.

First of all, as you're making your practice tosses to the outside, give yourself a little height so you can move into position if need be. Two or three feet over your head should be about maximum.

Let's say your toss is going to land to your side, but a little in front or behind you. Turn your body, get your weight onto the flexed support leg and take the kick. Don't forget to lean away to get that balanced stance. If the toss is off to your side but too far in or away, just take a shuffle step in the appropriate direction, lean away and bring your foot up.

Think of your kicks as strokes you learn. When the footbag is coming down off kilter in some way, you want to move your whole body into position to take the right "stroke". You don't want to root yourself in one position and then be forced to take strange kicks.

All right. Enough coaching. Work on this kick by yourself or with a partner. Go through it deliberately, try to bump the footbag either straight into the air (when you're practicing solo) or in an arc when you're with a partner. Remember not to swing or bat at the footbag. The motion is a lift.

SOME BEGINNING GAMES

You're tired of practicing. You've gotten to the point where you're frequently able to get a foot on the footbag and occasionally it even pops up like it's supposed to.

You're hot.

So what's next.

The best place to go with your newly developed expertise is to a "Hacky-circle" and the ideal number to get together is four. Everyone stands together in a square and the idea is to pass the footbag around foot-to-foot-to-foot-to-foot. There are only two rules:

(1) The word "sorry" is prohibited. There are no apologies in this game. If, on the remote chance you muff an easy one, and feel you have to say something, talk about gravity warps, tricky winds, specks of dirt in your eye...things like that. Or just glare at them all. It works for me.

(2) If you pick up a downed footbag, you have to start the next pass with a "courtesy toss" to someone else in the circle.

The nicest thing about "Hacky-circles" is that you don't have to be all that accurate with your kicks. No matter how it flies off your foot (assuming you've gotten a little height to it) it'll be to *some*one. If you like, and if the rest of the players are willing to believe you, you can take credit for some really awful kicks.

Note: If one of your players is particularly quick of foot, you can locate him in the center of the circle and try to route all your passes through him. The climbers in Yosemite call this "Banzai Hacky" and it'll definitely keep the man in the middle on his toes.

CONSECUTIVE KICKS

I've deliberately put off a discussion of consecutives until now because everybody has a tendency to start them too soon, before they have a chance to really isolate their kicks and work out the bugs. If neither your Inside or Outside kicks are even semi-reliable, any effort at consecutives is pretty foredoomed and the frustration could drive even a Zen master to petty acts of self-violence.

So I'll begin with a warning: Even though it's not as exciting, practice your kicks one at a time until they start to pop up with some regularity. You can do this by yourself, or with a partner, but do it.

I speak to you with the authority of painful experience.

Having said that, I'll move on to the topic at foot.

Solo consecutive kicks are a "Hacky-Sacker's" personal scoring system. They can warp normal personalities into compulsive kick counters very quickly. As a motivator for improving your game they are unmatched.

Following are a few pointers to launch you into the numbers game.

(1) Don't use your toe kick if you can avoid it at all. Jump out there and make your saves with a control kick, Inside or Outside. And don't use your knee if you can help it either. Back off and take in-close shots with an Inside Kick.

(2) Concentrate as much as you can on alternating feet.

(3) Think of your kicks as bunts, and make them soft. Keep the height of your kicks between your waist and just above your head.

(4) A lot of people find it easier to start with Inside Kicks while walking. It seems to prevent the footbag from bouncing into their upper body.

(5) If you get stuck somewhere in the low teens, or in the high single digits, (typical), start out from 100 and count backwards so you'll end up with tallies like 88 or 91. Does wonders for the confidence.

(6) *When To Take What Kick*. If you're like 99% of the world's population, you've got one good foot and one lame-brain. For most of us that works out to mean we're right-footed. Our Inside Right is better than our Inside Left; ditto for our Outsides. And during the practice sessions it seems like it's asking too much to complicate an already difficult motion by trying it with your weird foot. And so you concentrate on your strength.

The result, though, is the lopsided kicker phenomenon. You'll go through unbelievable contortions to try to get your good foot on a pass that really ought to be taken with your other side. And sometimes you'll make these incredible pretzel saves, but you know you can't go on like this. "Hacky Sackers" are two-footed animals, you've got to bring you bad foot up to par.

The first thing you ought to do to further this cause is to take every courtesy toss with your bad side. And when you're practicing by yourself, start out the same way. Force yourself to go with your bad side even though it's depressing at first. Persevere.

If you want, use a tennis analogy for a second. Think of your bad side as your backhand; you just can't play the game without it.

Back to the original topic of this section, when to take what kicks.

As I've mentioned before, your Inside Kick is meant to be taken when the footbag is dropping between your shoulders and just in front of you. The Outside Kick is meant to be taken whenever the footbag is dropping outside your shoulders and beside you. In addition, right-side kicks ought to be taken whenever the flight path of the footbag has taken it over to the right side of an imaginary center line drawn on your body. For the left side kicks it works just the opposite.

Now, if you were a statue you might not be able to play very exciting footbag games, but it would certainly be easy to tell which kick to take. Given the fact though that you're constantly moving, it's not so easy. As a general rule of thumb, do this: If you can turn and step into a pass, take it on an Inside Kick, left or right, depending on its direction. If it's too far away for that, turn and take it on one of your Outside Kicks. Stay light on your feet and you'll be amazed at what you can get to.

With just these two kicks and the ability to take them on both sides, you'll be able to hold your own in most any "Hacky-Circle", and you might even get into the double digits on your solo consecutives.

You'll also be ready for the next stage.

STEP FOUR: The Back Kick

This is the glamour kick, the very flashy looking last second save that'll extend your range and also give you an offensive weapon in net-sack. Look at the illustration for the basic idea.

The Back Kick is usually called upon to reach a footbag that is moving pretty quickly, either directly at you, or arching over you and headed for the stands. There is no time to back up and take an Inside, or slide back and take an Outside. The situation calls for drastic action.

The motion for the Back Kick shares a lot in common with the Outside Kick. Once again you'll be shifting your weight entirely onto your support leg, but this time you'll be lifting up your foot *behind* you. At the same time you'll have to turn your upper body both to keep an eye on the footbag and maybe to get out of the way too.

I recognize this is a lot of description for just one motion. Try it though before you throw up your hands. Some things are a lot easier done than said.

A few pointers to keep in mind:

(1) Use your lead arm to balance yourself and move your trailing arm out of the way, so that it doesn't obstruct your balance or vision.

(2) Keep your kicking foot *flat*. Use the same spot on the outside of your foot as you did for the Outside Kick.

This is probably the hardest kick to practice by

When you're first starting out, it's critical that your partner throw you nice easy tosses that are accurately placed for each kick. You shouldn't have to stretch or jam up for any of them.

yourself, so try to round up a partner to help you. If you're passing back and forth, start every effort with a courtesy toss to your (or his) back kick. The placement of this toss is critical. You shouldn't have to stretch or jam up for it. It should go a foot or so over your shoulder with just enough force to put it on the ground a long stride behind you. As soon as the footbag passes over your shoulder, you should shift your weight forward as you're bringing up your kicking foot. Meanwhile, in order to keep an eye on the footbag, you'll be turning your head and upper body.

When it's finally mastered, it's a mightily impressive kick. The footbag is past your body, the audience is headed for the exits, but then, suddenly, it's back in play.

Amazing.

And later, when you can make consistent contact, you can use this kick for some real velocity in net-sack.

For now though, just concentrate on the basics. Like every other kick the temptation is to come up too early. You'll meet it with your ankle or miss it entirely. Think "bunt" and come up slowly, making contact late. (If your friend's tosses don't let you hit them late and low, get him to change.)

A Final Note: The Back Kick and the Outside Kick are cousins not only in the sense that their motion is similar, but they also "merge" at some point off your rear quarter. A "true" Back Kick is directly behind you; and a "true" Outside Kick is directly off to your side, but the area in-between is shared between the two. Probably the best way to practice your Back Kick is to work backwards from your Outside, going through the shared zone until you're finally able to make good contact all the way back to a point directly behind you.

ADVANCED STUFF

In the rarefied air of advanced footbag games, the biggest change is speed. The footbag is not lofted anymore, it's rifled. In net-sack particularly, where spikes and whip-shot back kicks are routine, there's little time for careful deliberation. For these special circumstances advanced kickers have developed "fliers", inside and outside kicks taken in mid-air, when there's no time to set properly. Needless to say, these kinds of kicks demand a great deal of experience and a razor-fine sense of timing. When they're mastered though, they can turn a casual back-and-forth game into an adrenalized fire-fight.

The official rules for net-sack play are available from the National Hacky-Sack players Association (see back page for address). Very briefly, the rules are very similar to volleyball rules except for the obvious change from hands to feet. In addition, each team is allowed 5 consecutive kicks before being required to put it over the net, and each individual player is allowed 3 consecutive kicks.

Net play requires a reasonable degree of competence among the players but by no means is it an experts only affair. In fact it provides an excellent opportunity to work on Back Kicks and for that reason alone, it's worth breaking your 4-man "Hacky-circle" into a net game now and then.

THE KLUTZ ENTERPRISES

Flying Apparatus Catalogue

Klutz Press is a specialist in the field of gravity defiance systems, and *The Hacky Sack Book* is actually our second venture into it. In 1977 we published *Juggling for the Complete Klutz*, and its subsequent success has enabled a nation of klutzes to come juggling out of their closets with some measure of pride and even flair.

The juggling book is written by Messrs. Cassidy and Rimbeaux and illustrated by Diane Waller, more or less the same team that produced this volume. In addition, the book is sold with three calico and denim bean bags attached, designed to be the ideal size and weight for juggling.

Now that you've sampled Hacky Sack and tasted the pleasures of gravity defiance, you might be interested in carrying the struggle even further. If so, we make *Juggling for the Complete Klutz* available through the mail (or you can find it at your local bookstore). We also sell bean bags by themselves, juggling pins, rings and other paraphernalia (and these you *can't* find at your local store). Use the order blank to order extra "Hacky Sacks," or any of our juggling items listed.

MAIL ORDER INFORMATION

The Hacky Sack Book $9.^{95}

A 72 page how-to book on
the fine art of Hacky Sack
footbag games. Written
by the same crew as
produced the best-
selling *Juggling for
the Complete Klutz.*
Packaged with
one Hacky
Sack footbag.

Footbags

Two-Panel Style $7.^{00}

Thirty-two gram, hand-stitched, all
leather, fully-patented, human-
powered, anti-gravity devices. Used
in the New American Footbag Games.
Designed for a lifetime of foot-propelled flying.

Multi-Panel Style $9.^{00}

Constructed from cowhide and
multi-panelled, these footbags are
the product of a great deal of
careful stitching.

Juggling for the Complete Klutz $9.⁹⁵

The most popular book on juggling ever published. A 65 page volume, written for the mashed-finger and dented-shin crowd. By John Cassidy & B.C. Rimbeaux. Illustrated by Diane Waller. Comes with with three juggling bags.

Juggling Bags $2.⁰⁰ ea. $5.⁰⁰ per set of 3

Colorful, hand-sewn bean bags of calico and denim . . . ideal size and weight for juggling. They don't bounce around, they won't roll away, and they won't make a mess on the floor. No klutz is complete without them.

Ultimate Juggling Bags $8.⁰⁰ per set of 3

Sewn with crushed red velour (instead of calico and denim). Appropriate for most formal occasions.

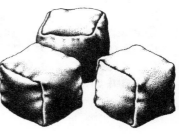

Juggling Pins $21.⁵⁰ per set of 3

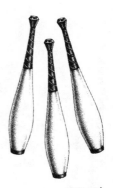

Three injection molded polyethylene juggling pins. Basically the same shape as bowling pins except they're balanced and designed for juggling. Red, blue, and yellow colors.

Professional Style Pins $49.⁵⁰ per set of 3

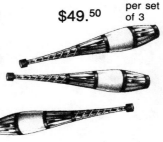

For the semi-serious juggler. Polyethylene construction, with a padded knob, bottom, extra handle and a two-tone gold and white finish. Barnum and Bailey material.

Juggling Balls $8.⁵⁰ per set of 3

Three lacrosse-style, hard rubber balls with a ribbed, easy-to-grip surface. Each set contains one red, one blue and one yellow ball.

Juggling Rings $15.⁰⁰ per set of 3

Manufactured for us, these are die-cut and smooth-machined out of polyethylene plastic. Indestructible, light and colorful, they are 13'' in outside diameter.
Sergei Ignatov, the Michael Jordan of juggling, always uses rings when keeping more than 11 objects going at once.

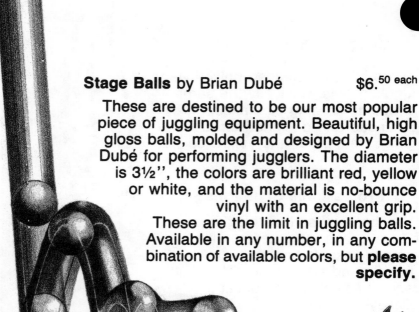

Stage Balls by Brian Dubé $6.$^{50 each}$

These are destined to be our most popular piece of juggling equipment. Beautiful, high gloss balls, molded and designed by Brian Dubé for performing jugglers. The diameter is 3½'', the colors are brilliant red, yellow or white, and the material is no-bounce vinyl with an excellent grip. These are the limit in juggling balls. Available in any number, in any combination of available colors, but **please specify.**

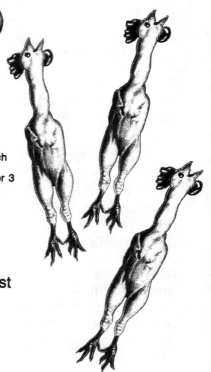

The Juggling Chicken $6.$^{00 each}$
                          $15.$^{00 for 3}$

We offer here aerodynamically sound polyvinyl poultry, with a style and flair that speak for themselves. You may use them for juggling, as decorations around your home or patio, or just for general household purposes.

MAIL ORDER BLANK

Quantity	Description	Price
	Add $1.00 for Postage	
	Total Enclosed (check or money order)	

Name _____

Street _____

Address _____

H   Klutz Enterprises / 2170 Staunton Ct. / Palo Alto CA 94306

FREE CATALOGUE FORM

The *FLYING APPARATUS CATALOGUE* is filled with unicycles, juggling paraphernalia, kites, boomerangs and who knows what all. It's available free for the asking.

Name _____

Street _____

Town/State _____

Zip _____

H

Please include check or money order and mail to:
Klutz Enterprises / 2170 Staunton Ct. / Palo Alto CA 94306

MAIL ORDER BLANK

Quantity	Description	Price
	Add $1.00 for Postage	
	Total Enclosed (check or money order)	

Name _____

Street _____

Address _____

H Klutz Enterprises / 2170 Staunton Ct. / Palo Alto CA 94306

FREE CATALOGUE FORM

The *FLYING APPARATUS CATALOGUE* is filled with unicycles, juggling paraphernalia, kites, boomerangs and who knows what all. It's available free for the asking.

Name _____

Street _____

Town/State _____

Zip _____

H

Please include check or money order and mail to:
Klutz Enterprises / 2170 Staunton Ct. / Palo Alto CA 94306

Where the players make the difference!

The World Footbag Association (WFA) was formed in 1983 to promote, educate, and stimulate interest in footbags, footbag games, and most importantly, the players who thrive on them. The WFA is the promotional arm behind the sport of footbag, and sponsors a number of activities, including tournaments, festivals, demonstrations, tours, training camps, and player workshops.

The WFA offers a lifetime membership to any player who wants to become better informed and more involved. This membership includes an official lifetime WFA membership card, a complimentary issue of the magazine *Footbag World*, a players' manual, and discounts of up to 50% on all WFA products and events.

To join, send $1.00 ($5.00 if you live outside the United States) along with your name, permanent address, phone number, date of birth and sex, to the address listed below. Please mention this publication as your reference.

The yearly subscription price for *Footbag World* **plus** a lifetime membership is only $5.00 ($15.00 if you live outside the United States). This magazine offers you all the latest in footbag products, upcoming events, coaching advice, tournament results, and much more.

JOIN THE WFA TODAY

World Footbag Association
1317 Washington Ave. Suite 7
Golden, Colorado 80401
(303) 278-9797